The Author's Edge

The Author's Edge

Marlene Mesot

Print layout, e-book conversion, and cover design by DLD Books

DLD Books

www.dldbooks.com
Editing and Self-Publishing Services

Cover photo by Marlene Mesot

© 2022 by Marlene Mesot
All rights reserved

ISBN: 978-1-7347393-2-9

4 Elements of Mystery Series

1. The Purging Fire
2. The Snowball Effect
3. Whirlwind of Fear
4. Terra Terror

More Mysteries

The Cat Stalker's Sonnets — novel

Poetry

Edgy Poetry
Deadly Poetry
The Author's Edge

www.marlsmenagerie.com

Dedication

This work is dedicated to all my friends and fellow writers who belong to Behind Our Eyes Writers' Group. Thank you sincerely for your constructive criticism, encouragement and true dedication to our writing craft. May God bless and productive writing.

Table of Contents

Dedication 7

Part I (2020)

Foreword 15
The Author's Edge 19
Writer's Instruments 20
Writer 21
The Movies 22
A Cloud 23
Inside a Book 24
Beginning To End 25
The Writer, Musician, Painter of Life 26
Running with a Story 27
This Author's Handiwork 29
The Author's Alphabet 31
Slant and Opposition 33
The Author's Words 34
Dear Author 35
Alliterative Genre 36
Tribute To Nonfiction 37
Weathering Life 38
The Storyteller's Ballad 39
Passion for Mystery 40
How To Cook Up a Mystery 41

Give Me a Limerick	43
Limericks	44
Poem	45
Start Your Day with a Poem	46
Poetry Is Music in Words	47
The Music of Poetry	48
Reader	49
Craft	50
Stories	51
Story Telling	52
Romances	53
Science Fiction	54
Summer Heat	55
Restore My Heart	56
Writer's Block	57
Mine	58
Write and Sing To Paint Life	59
Who Is the Greatest Author?	60
Where Do Ideas Come From?	61
The Author	62

Part II (2021)

Preface	67
God Spoke His Word	69
Ideas Taunt	70
Thoughts	71
How To Influence Your Writing	72
The Work of Writing	73
The Art of Writing	74
Improvise with Muster	75
Moniker	76
I Don't Blog	77

With Luck	78
Train Your Brain	79
Word Connection	80
Play with Words	81
Word Play	82
Think Homonyms	83
If This Were a Book	84
Look at a Book	85
Learn from Books	86
What's in a Book Cover	87
Questions	88
Mystery Spiral	89
Storytelling	90
Building Your Story	91
Story to Poem	92
Poem	93
A Poem a Day	94
Branching Poetry	95
Hunt Down All Your Poems	96
My Poetry Folders	97
What Is a Limerick	98
How To Write a Limerick	99
When You Write a Limerick	100
Where Do Limericks Come From?	101
Who Should Write a Limerick?	102
Why Write Limericks	103
This Manuscript	104
Open Up To Writing	105
Story Funnel	106
Ode To Original Writing	107
The Last Poem	108

Part I (2020)

My heart overflows with a good theme; I address my verses to the King; My tongue is the pen of a ready writer.

Psalm 45:1
New American Standard Bible

Foreword

by Lynda McKinney Lambert

Marlene Mesot's readers will connect with her newest collection of forty poems from the opening quatrain of her first poem, "The Author's Edge."

It is not a surprise that the format of this collection is well-organized and has a clear focus because Mesot's academic background includes a bachelor's degree in education and a MA degree in Library and Information Studies. Beneath the title at the top of each poem, she includes the name of the form for that particular poem. The poems cover various formats, such as quatrain, quintet, couplet, limerick, and more. Because the poet provides the additional information, it gives the reader insight that is usually not available in a book of poetry. It also gives the author an educational edge at the same time as it connects with the reader.

Mesot clarifies her intention that her "verses are a gift to the King," as she quotes from Psalm 45.1.

The opening poem is "The Author's Edge," and she introduces the poet's concept as a crafter who works with body and mind simultaneously.

Craftsmanship in the arts is a recurring theme that appears consistently.

This poem reminded me of Italian Renaissance sculptor, painter, writer, architect, and poet, Michelangelo. As a sculptor who influenced the development of Western art, he described his search for the unseen forms inside the marble blocks.

She writes,

> Only the crafter sees the stages it takes
> As it forms into work worth its keep...
> Elements are combined in a cohesive state.
> To make it memorable...

Several poems address weaving. From the beginning to the end of this collection of poetry, Mesot seems to be weaving ideas and actions:

> Plot is the thread pulling the story.
> Actions are the events pushing the worry.
> Solution is the cloth of the tapestry.

In the trident poem "The Writer, Musician, Painter of Life," she continues using imagery signifying the use of the arts,

> ...the fabric of life is woven.

As in the poem "Alliterative Genre," weaving merges with the use of voice.

> Weave it with wisdom and wit.
> Always this author's voice will be heard.

She emphasizes the importance of speaking and declares that the voice is "The author's Handiwork."

She works her way through this series of poems using a wide range of poetic formats. It feels like she is conscientiously continuing to weave her way along the path she established from the inception of this book.

In her quatrain "Inside a Book," she declares that as you read a book, you will "see beyond your eyes to immersion." She eventually discloses her encounter with her intention of celebrating the imagination.

> Let your imagination bond
> With the story as it moves along
> Go beyond your own life
> Inside the pages of a book.

And here we discover the invitation to go on a journey with the poet.

In the quatrain "Running with a Story," she tells us she

> ...ran without
> Knowing where I was going.

Another favorite poem for me is "The Author's Alphabet," because she so clearly shows how to structure the poem as well as how to use that structure to express the message. I love to write Abecedarian poems.

For Marlene Mesot, music associates with words, and this is an idea that becomes the title of her poem "Poetry is Music in Words" in another quatrain.

> Music's telling is in the note.
> Poetry's voice is in the words spoke.

Singing, voice, and painting become the focus in her poem "Restore My Heart."

> A song speaks...
> A poem speaks...
> A painting remains vivid in time.

Our journey with Marlene Mesot ends at this location, where we discover that the end was really introduced as we entered into the hidden message of the collection of poems.

"Write and Sing To Paint Life." This is my favorite poem.

> Art is the vision of beauty.
> All blend to make life whole.

Seeing takes time. It requires patience.

Clarity comes slowly. It's not a quick glance and a fast stride.

These poems open up and reveal things that were partially hidden at the beginning of this journey.

~ Lynda McKinney Lambert
Award winning Artist and Author: *Songs for the Pilgrimage, Star Signs, First Snow, Walking by Inner Vision.*

The Author's Edge

(Quatrain)
07/31/2020

Of this trade words are the tools.
The page is the work bench.
Plot twists are the pools
That will the story entrench.

With wisdom and care it takes shape.
Style is the means that makes it unique.
Only the crafter sees the stages it takes
As it forms into a work worth its keep.

Each character is placed with care.
Each scene builds to make it complete.
Setting has its place without flare.
Each story becomes an amazing feat.

Elements are combined in a cohesive state.
To make it memorable is the author's pledge.
The finished work a unique project will make.
All these parts bring the whole to the author's edge.

Writer's Instruments

(Quintet)
08/06/2020

Paper, pens, erasers rest
All upon the writer's desk.
Writer's instruments lay.
They have all gone away.
Now computer, printer best?

Writer

(Acrostic)
07/24/2020

Willing to seek out new ideas,
Ready to explore,
Initialize new beginnings,
To boldly go where no one has gone before,
Engage new concepts,
Reach for the final frontier and beyond.

The Movies

(Couplet)
07/05/2020

Think of your favorite movie,
The one you thought really groovy.

Now bring to bear,
The one that gave you a scare.

Then think of one of passion,
Or one you thought in fashion.

One that gave you a chill,
Or one that gave you a thrill.

The epic is there, but just be aware,
To the book they can never compare.

A Cloud

(Limerick)
07/04/2020

A cloud is just a vapor,
A wispy thought, a taper.
It withers away.
Never more to stay,
Unless it's pressed to paper.

Inside a Book

(Quatrain)
08/06/2020

Open the pages of a book,
Swipe on your tablet. Take a look.
Put on your earphones for the audio version,
See beyond your eyes to immersion.

Immerse yourself inside a book.
Fall in love with the story. It's a hook.
Get to know the characters lives.
Follow the plot. Feel its vives.

Let your imagination bond
With the story as it moves along.
Go beyond your own life, look,
Inside the pages of a book.

Beginning To End

(Trident)
07/28/2020

In the beginning an idea surfaces.
By the middle its problem flourishes.
At the end a solution emerges.

In the beginning characters emerge.
By the middle problems surge.
At the end evil purge.

Plot is the thread pulling the story.
Actions are the events pushing the worry.
Solution is the cloth of the tapestry.

The Writer, Musician, Painter of Life

(Trident)
05/21/2011

Capture that thought, that note,
The brush stroke,
Before they fly.

Hold onto the idea, grasp it firmly,
But hold it tenderly,
Until in hand are your tools.

To begin, tap that keyboard. Dab your brush.
Tune that instrument, for the right touch,
As the fabric of life is woven.

Whether 'tis yours alone,
Or made to be shown,
It remains your masterpiece anywhere.

Treasure your gift of fragrance rare.
You are unique, beyond compare.
Your gift is as unique as our Creator.

Running with a Story

(Quatrain)
09/03/2020

I was a pantser no doubt.
I took an idea and ran without
Knowing where I was going.
I just took it and started roaming,

That I was a pantser is true.
I ran with a story not knowing what to do.
I knew what the end result would be,
But how to get there was a mystery to me.

Into my story I went,
Without much thought or repent.
Once I got to the middle,
I just started to fiddle.

I left it there,
Only to stare.
How could I not know,
Where I was to go?

I knew where I wanted to end,
But couldn't get round that bend,
It seemed like a very long track,
Until I found my way back.

Marlene Mesot

There are three simple parts to a story,
Beginning, middle, end. No worry.
Start small with a simple plan,
Then add elements to expand.

Start with a person or plot,
Add obstacles to stir the pot.
Add emotion as food for thought.
Keep the tension taught.

Whether fiction or truth you write,
They both share characteristics of might.
A hook sparks interest in the reader.
A unique theme makes you a leader.

Show me the story again.
Let me feel it beginning to end.
Don't stop when you haven't got a clue.
Maybe someone will write a review!

This Author's Handiwork

(Alliterative Quatrain)
08/19/2020

Write me a work worthy of many a wonderful word.
Weave it with wisdom and wit.
Always this author's voice will be heard,
Quickened with quote and quip.

Tell me a tale from yesterday or today.
Take me to another time, another place.
Tantalize it with settings far away.
Let the mood set the pace.

Sprinkle in splendid setting.
Supple it showing surprising suspense.
Who finds the creatures worth petting?
Who rides the rim of the fence?

Create characters so completely conceived,
They become vivid and real to engage.
They bring life and flavor to be believed,
Transcending the work on the page.

Perfect a plot particular and privy
To this author's handiwork
Dish up dialogue dirty or ditty
That reveals this author's quirk.

Entwine emotion evaluating the evidence,
Pour in passion anew,
Weave the work with skillful diligence,
Carefully crafting each clue.

From fact or from fiction a story gets its fate.
No matter the work, they use the same tools.
Paint a picture perfectly balanced in weight.
This author makes up the rules.

This author's handiwork is hopefully heavy
With unique style and grace.
Anticipating the readers' attention to aptly levy.
Tugging the tapestry in place.

You, dear author, imagine and anticipate,
Steering the story along.
Blending with beauty, hoping readers appreciate,
This author's handiwork. Come! Belong!

The Author's Alphabet

(Abecedarian)
08/11/2020

A — accentuates the author, among constant things.
B — brings a book into being, the state that life brings.

C — conjures character, casting the players..
D — designates draft, first of many layers.

E — ever erasing, a constant fix.
F — focuses on fiction, throwing tales into the mix.

G — governs glossary, at the end of a book.
H — yes, you guessed it! H is for hook.

I — inspires insight, intuition from inside.
J — stands for juvenile, but some kids are wise.

K — connotes keeping your story going strong.
L — leads to length, whether short or long.

M — remembers memoir, mystery and more.
N — the needed notebook, a keepsake for sure.

O — opens opinion of which there will be many.
P — proports the paper, pens, pencils, paints. Tools vary.

Q — queries questions, many and wide.
R — is you dear reader, a book's heart and pride.

S — spans synopsis, summarizing your story in brief.
T — talents telling stories, an art tradition to keep.

U — is for you, a euphemism at best.
V — values variety, the ultimate test.

W — the wise writer, and word, the ultimate tool.
X — expresses example, to illustrate the rule.

Y — is for yesterday, when your story was due.
Z — your zest and zeal, to make it bright and new.

There are many ways to bring the author's alphabet to light.
Why don't you try it? Give it all your might!

Slant and Opposition

(Sonnet)
08/25/2020

What determines your position,
Is how you slant your petition.
Some welcome water wonderfully wet,
Others fear it with utter detest.

Snowflakes cover all things white and cold.
Some fear falling. Some play joyous, bold.
Some folks say their piece with ease.
Some folks bully, taunt and tease.

Each one has a way with word,
Giving meaning or absurd.
What some might like, others detest.
How you say it influences best.

Authors write and rant.
All depends on slant.

The Author's Words

(Trident)
10/07/2020

Measure your words, simple and true.
Write me a piece, just for us two.
Let it flow free, timeless and new.

Author, my clever friend, bringing
Life to your words. Give them meaning.
Bring your masterpiece into being.

Concepts within, words flow without,
Fashion it well, what you're about.
What will it tell, inside and out?

Dear Author

(Quatrain)
07/22/2020

Make me believe
In the story that you weave.
Where fact and fiction blend
It will be timeless until the end.

Let the excitement flow
From tales of long ago.
Bring me the action of a thriller
Not necessarily with a killer.

Whether science fiction or science fact
Make it rich with impact.
If a fantasy let me dwell
Under the words of your spell.

Make me believe
In the ideas you retrieve.
Thoughtful ponderence for fodder
As I read Dear Author.

Alliterative Genre

(Quatrain)
08/11/2020

Black as dark, global thriller abides.
Blue, changeable as the sky, suspense adds surprise.
Red, as blood, weaves a trail of mystery.
Brown, as the earth, cleave the stages of history.

Yellow, bright as the sun, shines in romances new.
Like green grass, growth sprinkles memoir through.
Orange, as spices bring holiday cheer.
Gray, as dusk, holds memories dear.

Pure as white snow nonfiction stands bold.
Purple as pedals fragrant, science fiction stories unfold.
Perfectly pink, ponders the phases of fantasy.
Color your world with ostentatious audacity.

Tribute To Nonfiction

(Sonnet)
08/16/2020

When you write a story's sleuth,
Do not think yourself aloof.
Nonfiction uses the same fare
As tools of fiction written with care.

The first sentence needs a hook,
To get readers to take a look,
As the rest of your piece unfolds,
Telling a true story bold.

Interest is a vital key,
To let readers really see,
The true meaning behind the words,
Bring life out of the absurd.

Truth is vital everywhere,
To get people to care.

Weathering Life

(Limerick)
08/10/2020

No one controls the weather.
Storms of life we must weather.
Words are writers' tools.
Writers make the rules.
Fact and fiction together.

The Storyteller's Ballad

(Ballad)
07/19/2020

A man set out on a quest.
He knew he had to try his best.
He wanted to pass his test,
To find a perfect story to tell a guest.

He observed many things—
Talked with peasants, queens, and kings.
But nothing had a true ring,
Of stories he might bring.

He searched far and wide,
Went to land, sea and sky,
Held onto his pride,
Yet his best story came from inside.

Passion for Mystery

(Limerick)
07/11/2020

Mystery is my passion.
It is always in fashion.
Ask why all the time.
With reason or rhyme.
Fill it with twists and action.

How To Cook Up a Mystery

(Sextet)
05/25/2011

You don't need a lesson in history
To learn how to construct a mystery.
Other authors in the genre read,
Including suspense, thriller and intrigue.
Romance and adventure add spice to the mix.
Don't forget to sprinkle in some plot twists.

Believable characters make a fiction work real.
They also decorate your book with appeal.
Populate your piece with plenty of suspects.
Make some of them as false witness.
Start with a hero, heroine and villain.
Surround them with people who will affect them.

Plot is the egg that binds your people together.
As yeast your plan makes all rise. Clever.
Once you roll out your puzzle, break it apart.
Questions with no answers is a great place to start.
Clues and false leads provide flavor in the mix.
By the time it is finished all have been fixed.

Set your table with care.
Placement and timing, are they all there?
Sequence of events, very important, it's true.
Add them with thought to your brew.

The mixture will thicken as you work it through.
Blend everything well for delicious proof.

A theme is your topping.
Lessons to learn add meaning.
Stir up a purpose
For an enjoyable reading.
Everyone has thoughts and ideas to share.
How you cook up your story makes it uniquely rare.

Give Me a Limerick

(Limerick)
08/25/2020

Give me a limerick please,
Of the rhyme scheme please take heed.
Wit and tactfully,
Catchy, wackily,
Flowing with rhythm and read.

Limericks

(Limerick)
12/03/2020

Limericks are five line poems.
Let's keep the rhythm going.
Tell it like it's true.
Just for me and you.
The meter here is showing.

Poem

(Limerick)
09/26/2020

Poem is a piece to perfect.
Rhyme scheme and meter project.
When thoughts go away,
Sit down in the hay,
No rhyme, no reason, no rest!

Start Your Day with a Poem

(Quatrain)
12/10/2020

Start your day with a poem.
Keep it short but flowing.
Express your heart all knowing,
That we love a good poem.

Poetry Is Music in Words

(Quatrain)
04/21/2020

Surely you have heard,
Poetry is music in words.
They both have rhythm. They both have rhyme.
But poetry's melody is of a different kind.

Surely you have heard,
Poetry is music in words.
Music's telling is in the note.
Poetry's voice is in the words spoke.

Surely you have heard,
Poetry is music in words.
Both rise and swell as the momentum grows.
What form it will take only the author knows.

The Music of Poetry

(Sonnet)
04/05/2020

Poetry is music in words.
Its melodic rhythm flows. Have you heard?
It speaks to your inner soul,
As its rhyme resoundingly tolls.

Its scheme can be patterned set like notes,
Or rhyme and rhythm there may be none. There's hope.
The music is the lyric,
Whether free verse or limerick.

A poem's pace is set by its rhythm.
Its virtual voice can be obvious or within hidden.
The tone of the poem sets the mood,
Whether shouted or subdued.

Thoughts become concepts of form.
There is no right or wrong way to a poem.

Reader

(Limerick)
11/30/2020

Reader, reader of the page.
Stories performed like on stage.
Let the story hook,
Interest in book.
Satisfaction to engage.

Craft

(Limerick)
12/03/2020

Craft your manuscript with care.
Thought and love belong in there.
Errors? You must look
Read it like a book.
When you're ready go and share!

Stories

(Limerick)
11/30/2020

Tall tales, fables, anywhere.
Tell your story with fan fare.
Stories told in brief.
Share them with relief.
From one to another share.

Story Telling

(Limerick)
11/30/2020

Throughout the old age of time.
Stories shared by reason, rhyme.
Stories one two three.
Shared with you and me.
Tell them, write them, pantomime.

Romances

(Acrostic Couplet)
07/22/2020

Recite words of love from your soul,
Only those that keep us whole,
Make me understand the breadth of our love,
According to the stars above,
Never shall we be apart,
Considering the connection of heart,
Emotions that will always ring true,
Since the time that I met you.

Science Fiction

(Limerick)
07/30/2020

Science fiction is not true.
Science fact may be there too.
Make it scary, more.
Give it passion, sure.
It could happen just for you.

Summer Heat

(Limerick)
07/19/2020

Day was hot, I could not breathe.
Humid air. It took no leave.
When ideas dry up.
Seems you have no luck.
Press on. Don't let anger peeve.

Restore My Heart

(Quatrain)
08/11/2020

Sing me a song most memorable.
Paint me a picture so true.
Write me stories plentiful.
Restore my heart light and new.

A song speaks in melody.
A poem speaks in rhyme.
My heart feels black as ebony.
A painting remains vivid in time.

Let me feel the song in my heart.
Let me hear the story in my mind.
Let me treasure the joy of painted parts.
To restore my heart's soul in time.

Writer's Block

(Sonnet)
07/30/2020

Once your story is half way there,
Then your ideas vanish into the air,
They appear to have all dried up,
Your writing instrument seems to be stuck.
Now there's nothing to take stock.
It's the symptoms of writer's block.

Oh my, now what will you do?
Can you sit and think the problem through?
Do not be worried and stress.
Let you mind ponder and write your best.
Some event will trigger the way
Take it step by step each day.

You can salvage work, no cost.
Writer's block, withstand the loss.

Mine

(Couplet)
07/22/2020

The blue of your eyes,
Holds the breadth of the skies.

The gold of your hair
So soft and rich is beyond compare.

Your hug makes me aware
Of the depth of your care.

The joy that you give,
Adds life as I live.

You trust and are kind,
Restoring my faith in the divine.

You are my treasure,
Bringing hope beyond measure.

The love that you bring,
Makes my heart want to sing.

You make my world brighter,
Are the words of this writer.

These words that I pen,
Will last beyond our end.

Write and Sing To Paint Life

(Quatrain)
09/06/2020

Tell me a story.
Write me a song.
Paint me a picture.
To last my life long.

Let the words touch me.
Let me hear the melody.
As each instance moves me.
Let me see the imagery.

Literature is the essence of life.
Music is the balm to the soul.
Art is the vision of beauty.
All blend to make life whole.

Who Is the Greatest Author?

(Couplet)
07/05/2020

Who is the greatest Author?
Christy, Dickens, Chaucer?

Is it a poet, journalist, storyteller?
Is it a woman or a feller?

It must be someone you admire,
Someone to whom you aspire.

In the world there are many it's true,
But who is important to you?

The greatest Author, of course,
Is the One from the Book of Hebrews verse.

Where Do Ideas Come From?

(Quatrain)
12/10/2020

Where do ideas come from?
That is the million dollar question.
From the recesses of the inner mind?
Or the Outer Limits of our expression?

When you think one thing, but write another,
When your words take on a mind of their own,
is this a trick of the brain, or something other
Than what you expected? You are not alone.

So open up that wayward, rambling mind.
To be ready and willing to explore.
In unlikely places is where you will find,
Ideas and concepts that will endure.

What are ideas and how do they come?
Ideas come in all shapes, sizes and form.
Be aware in order not to lose them, forlorn.
It's where you take them after they're born.

The Author

(Quatrain)
04/13/2008

Is it just a fantasy?
Or can people really see
A glimpse of their reality
Through me.

A touch, a though, a word and then,
My story comes to life deepened.
By line let me set apart
Writing with a heart.

Writer, where's your motive lie?
Can you hold their interest high?
You view life with a verbal eye.
Audience identify.

Words and concepts play their parts
In writing meant to reach to hearts.
The power of the word still stands
To reach woman and man.

Is it just a fantasy?
Or a true glimpse of reality.
A touch, a thought, a word apart,
Writing with a heart.

Writer, where's your motive lie?
Audience identify.
The power of His Word still stands
To reach woman and man.

First published: *The Writer's Grapevine: SAMHAIN Edition*, Patty L. Fletcher, Ed. (Oct. 2020).

Part II (2021)

Therefore, since we have so great a cloud of witnesses surrounding us, let us also lay aside every encumbrance and the sin which so easily entangles us, and let us run with endurance the race that is set before us, fixing our eyes on Jesus, the author and perfecter of faith, who for the joy set before Him endured the cross, despising the shame, and has sat down at the right hand of the throne of God.

Hebrews 12:1–2
New American Standard Bible

Preface
07/19/2021

Originally, *The Author's Edge* was going to be a chapbook with 40 poems. However, another year has commenced, another April poetry month has come and gone, and creativity continues. So, I have decided to combine my efforts into two parts, which are 2020 and 2021 for one work. Consequently, when I sent the original to Lynda seeking a jacket review, she had no idea of the expansion of this project. Her evaluation is of the first part, hence this explanation of part two.

I hope you will enjoy this in its entirety. Even more than that, I hope this will motivate and inspire, both writers and readers, to look inside, and bring out your best self.

With love and sincerity,
Author Marlene Mesot

God Spoke His Word

(Quatrain)
11/07/2021

In the beginning God said,
God spoke the world into being.
His Word became flesh,
For us to behold by seeing.

He is the Author of our faith.
His Word is our bond.
He writes our names in His Book,
If we reach to Him, not beyond.

Psalms, parables and more,
To us He has given,
Left us with examples
For us to make the decision.

He has written His commandments in stone.
He has given us free will and choice.
His plan has been set in motion.
Can we now hear His voice?

Ideas Taunt

(Progressive by Stanza)
11/07/2021

As ideas taunt,
They become a prompt,
Urging me to action,
To my joy, satisfaction.

Let your ideas lurk.
Put your brain to work.
When you get a notion,
Put ideas into motion.

If it's good write it down.
It need not to be profound.
Just write out to what you attest.
Then go on with a piece to perfect.

Do not let it be haunting,
Just go do what you are wanting,
Let the lot of ideas come and go,
And let the good and bad ones ebb and flow.

Thoughts

(Quatrain)
07/05/2021

Sometimes thoughts come
While you are lying in bed.
But when they hit the paper,
They're different than in your head.

Thoughts come fleetingly
As vapor appears in the air.
For an instant you have them.
Then they are no longer there.

Keep repeating them over to yourself,
Until you get them to the page still alive,
Making them concrete and permanent,
Only then will they survive.

How To Influence Your Writing

(Ballad)
07/30/2021

Whether you are writing fiction or fact,
You must first do your research and that is that,
Unless you come at it from personal experience,
Then you can plan your piece forth hence.

When casting characters be inquisitive,
Take from facts a derivative,
List things about characters you have in mind,
This will act on your subconscious over time.

When plotting have it all worked out,
Know your story inside and out,
Like a puzzle you then pick it apart,
So your readers will be surprised from the start.

The sum of all parts make a whole,
But you piece it together very slow,
Let your notes work on your mind,
As you craft your story over time.

Determine what genre you want it to be,
Fantasy, romance, mystery?
How to influence your writing,
Can be an experience exciting

The Work of Writing

(Quatrain)
10/02/2021

Make no mistake.
You must concentrate.
There is work to writing,
But it is a task exciting.

There is work in penning words.
This concept is not absurd.
It is art like painting and music.
Express yourself. Do not lose it.

When you expose yourself vulnerable,
Then your writing will fulfill,
The hard won work of success,
For we all will be enriched and blessed.

The Art of Writing

(Quatrain)
07/28/2021

This project began as a chapbook,
But the subject soon became a hook,
Upon which new ideas were hung.
About writing there is much to be sung.

Writing is a rainbow of thought,
To which a myriad of color can be brought.
Its embodiment is vast as the ocean,
Ebbing and flowing with constant emotion.

Touch your writing instrument to paper.
Tap on keys so as not to lose words to vapor.
The art is to capture your audience with your words,
To touch them in a way they have never heard.

Each writer has a unique talent,
A way to present words that is different.
The writer controls the pace like an artist's brush,
Fulfilling ideas, crafting the piece with no rush.

Improvise with Muster

(Sextet)
05/11/2021

Improvisation is an actor's tool.
To improvise a plot is a mystery's rule.
How to plan without my demise,
A plot that is twisty and wise,
Is an undertaking with muster,
That must be performed without blunder.

Moniker

(Progressive by Stanza)
07/05/2021

It seems so lame,
To use your name,
To stake your claim,
To show your fame.

If this should come about,
For you without a doubt,
How could you stand out?
To show what you're about.

I choose to have a menagerie,
In this there is no tragedy,
It's not a display of pageantry,
It is just my own imagery.

There is no trick to this,
Just choose a brand and stick,
To show your moniker it fits,
For what you stand no risk.

Tell me what you have to say,
Make it yours in your own way,
You can be just what you portray,
So stand up and stand out today!

I Don't Blog

(Trident)
07/08/2021

I don't blog.
It seems like a bog,
To what I am about.

What can I say,
In another way,
That hasn't been written about?

Blogging takes time,
Not just in rhyme,
To sort your thoughts out.

Words I do not fudge,
So please do not judge,
What I am talking about.

There is much work,
It is no quirk,
To plan a blog out.

Once this blogging bottle is open,
It keeps on flowing, this notion,
Best to let it sort itself out.

To those bloggers who do,
Your talent is true,
Keep on what you are about!

With Luck

(Quatrain)
04/13/2021

I tried to write a pantoum form poem,
Guess I didn't know where I was going.
You see I had no luck,
Because I messed up the construct.

Sometimes with rhythm and meter,
I take liberties. Am I a cheater?
On only one aspect I would dwell.
I did not know the pattern well.

I tried to write a limerick,
But i had too many lines to make it stick.
So I kept practicing,
Even though it was taxing.

When you make a mistake, persevere.
Learning is why we are all here.
Now, with luck, limericks I can spit out.
But that is not all that I am about.

Train Your Brain

(Progressive by Word)
08/22/2021

Train your brain,
Train in this refrain,
Write about what you read,
Do like what you write indeed,
Practice makes writing ease come your way
So don't be afraid to practice every day.

Word Connection

(Trident)
Written 05/05/2021
Revised 09/04/2021

Words and impressions
Form a connection,
That bring our stories to life.

By turning the gears
Between words and ideas,
The plot sharpens to your ears.

Shaped by your ears,
Have no fears,
Keep your ideas.

From thought to paper,
No longer a vapor,
Write to your Maker.

No fear of rejection,
Keep making word connection,
Toward your goal of publication.

Play with Words

(Progressive by Word)
11/07/2021

What can I do,
To write something new?
As I play with the words,
I must not make it absurd.

As I play with words,
Is there something I heard?
What in the world could it be,
This new thing that possesses me.

Hurry up, write it down,
This new idea that I found.

Word Play

(Decastich)
11/07/2021

Ixnay,
Amscray,
Wordplay.

Don't look in your purse.
What can there be worse,
Than a nonsense verse?

Words are like music,
So do not lose it.
Let sounding notes shout,
What you are about!

Think Homonyms

(Quatrain)
04/12/2021

Go to the sync.
Don't even blink.
Wish out your song.
Let it flow strong.

Go to the sink.
Don't even think.
Water runs true.
Clean through and through.

Do not think of whether,
Your work has a measure.
Just write it for pleasure.
It will be your treasure.

Do not think of weather,
Control there is none never.
Control you can't endeavor.
Changes are forever.

If This Were a Book

(Progressive by Stanza)
07/06/2021

Take a look,
In a book.
You will see,
Such wonderful imagery.

What a rare flight,
Into wonder, heartache, insight,
Await the reader there,
The author's mindful fair.

If this were a book,
Hidden inside a small nook,
To answer all your questions,
Without any kind of interjections.

If this were a book,
I'd tell you to look,
Inside its pages to find,
The treasures it holds inside.

A book can take you places,
And introduce you to new faces.
It expands the reaches of minds,
And transcends the annals of time.

Look at a Book

(Progressive by Stanza)
04/02/2021

I took
A look.
No rook
A book.

Just laying around
What I found
Inside there bound
Was very profound.

Seems i was hooked
To read this book.
Sat in a nook
To take a look.

What wonders would there await?
There could be no mistake.
Chance not to miss out,
On what it is about.

Learn from Books

(Progressive by Stanza)
07/06/2021

We learn,
From books,
To discern,
The truth.

We must know,
Where to go,
How to grow,
What to show.

Learn to listen,
Sort it through,
Fact from fiction,
What is true.

Then we must trust,
To put into practice,
Our new instincts found,
What we shall master.

What's in a Book Cover

(Ekphrastic)
04/18/2021

What's in a book cover?
How many words does it convey?
How does it capture the imagination?
Influence the buying of it in any way?

It must convey the action,
The intent that is inside,
It should convey the author's premise,
The central theme to not hide.

The art of the book cover
Is to grab the reader's attention.
It needs to display the message
Of the author's intention.

Questions

(Quatrain)
11/07/2021

Let me shout WOW!
How many poems do I have now?
Are there enough for a collection?
Have I written them to perfection?

What is the question?
How many should I mention?
When we ask why,
How much air fills the sky?

With each breath that we take,
How many decisions can we make?
How long should we write?
Far into the night?

Life is about choices
So express your many voices.
Do not question or deny,
Born to write, you and I.

Mystery Spiral

(Ballad)
07/28/2021

Mystery arouses curiosity,
And invites questioning.
It evokes imagination,
And confounds reckoning.

Mystery says, "I can't find my pet. He or she is missing!"
Suspense adds, "My pet has a medical condition needing
 treatment and care, I am wishing."
Thriller appends, "My pet's condition may be transmissible
 to people in town, state, the world in general!"
From mystery, to suspense, to thriller is a spiral, a widening
 funnel!

Storytelling

(Sonnet)
07/08/2021

Please tell me you're not in a hurry,
'Cause I want to tell you a story,
It will not take up much of your time,
It's not a complex tale to unwind.

If all stories are universal,
Surely there is not a hurdle,
You can listen to a tale or two,
The choice is really all up to you.

Your interest is half the battle,
If you like tales that shake and rattle,
Your perception and reflection then,
Let the complicated tale begin.

I'll tell you one and then you will know,
If my storytelling has a flow.

Building Your Story

(Progressive by Stanza)
11/15/2021

Start with notes.
Take a look.
Story builds.
Set the hook.
As you plan,
Your new book.

Story too long,
What can you do?
Split into parts,
That's nothing new.
Where to divide?
You think it through.

Building a series,
How to reveal it?
What steps do you plan?
Do you conceal it?
Series are long term.
Set up and tell it.

The building blocks of stories,
Are numerous it is true.
Carefully set them in place,
As carefully you think through,
How each step is to play out,
To show your cohesion new.

Story to Poem

(Quatrain)
07/13/2021

Write me a story,
Then make it a poem.
No need to worry,
You are not alone.

Take an idea, but make it short.
Flash Fiction is your first resort.
From concept to narrative your story forms.
Then into verse it transforms.

Let your ideas swirl around,
Until the right rhythm you have found.
Story and poem are not so diverse.
From one to the other, just practice, rehearse.

Poem

(Haiku)
04/29/2021

A poem is a breath.
To each life it does attest.
A poem has a life.

A Poem a Day

(Quatrain)
04/01/2021

Does a poem a day
Keep the doctor away?
Not necessarily.
Not even warily.

Does a poem a day
Keep worries at bay?
No, not ever.
Not even clever.

Does a poem a day
Lead me astray?
No, it keeps the mind healthy,
And all my words wealthy.

Branching Poetry

(Quatrain)
07/06/2021

As roots extend from their tree,
Poetry pours out of me.
It flows like the ocean,
Once the bottle is open.

Its rhythm ebbs and flows,
As the tide comes and goes.
Never knowing where words will land,
Like leaves from branches expand.

It starts with a line,
Intending to rhyme,
It grows even more,
Like trees on the forest floor.

Trees provide shade,
Relief from our day.
Poetry expands our mind,
As trees withstand time.

Hunt Down All Your Poems

(Ballad)
09/06/2021

No mountain is too high,
No valley is too deep,
To search for a poem,
That I wanted to keep.

I will capture those words,
Whether on sticky note, napkin or paper,
To save for posterity.
Off my mission will not taper.

Save all you write,
No matter what your thought.
Whether it is good or bad,
The sentiment must not be lost.

Hunt down all your poems,
Gather these nuggets you treasure.
Let them be read,
For they deserve full measure.

Keep all your work,
Whether it brings you pain or pleasure.
Each one's talent is unique.
Develop it at your leisure.

My Poetry Folders

(Progressive by Word)
04/25/2021

In my fist,
I have a list,
Of all my poetry folders.
It's a burden off my shoulders.

But it may expand,
Beyond scope of my hand,
As I try to be clever,
While adding to this fascinating new endeavor.

Count words in this block,
To store up in your crock,
This is just my way to say,
Why not try writing a poem every day?

What Is a Limerick

(Limerick)
11/04/2021

What is a limerick poem?
Do you know where you're going?
Do not make it mean.
Keep it short and clean.
The rhythm keep it flowing.

How To Write a Limerick

(Limerick)
08/12/2021

How to write a limerick,
Think of rhythm, rhyme it quick,
Let your feelings go,
Let the rhythm flow,
Now you know the secret trick!

When You Write a Limerick

(Limerick)
09/06/2021

When you write a limerick,
Let it flow and make it stick.
Rhythm is the key.
Craft it patiently.
Keep it clean and nice, no trick.

Where Do Limericks Come From?

(Limerick)
11/02/2021

Where do limericks come from?
Are they born or are they spun,
From inside with care,
Give them love and flair,
Let them flow and let them run.

Who Should Write a Limerick?

(Limerick)
11/04/2021

Who should write a limerick
Anyone who knows the trick.
Five lines to the flow.
Rhythm you must know.
Clean ones do not make me sick.

Why Write Limericks

(Limerick)
11/04/2021

The five double U's are here.
Who what, when why, where no fear.
Number six is how.
Give it clout and wow.
Why? Limericks are so clear.

This Manuscript

(Progressive by Word)
07/06/2021

Thoughts become words.
Words turn into sentences.
Then they all come together,
To complete this manuscript's cohesive endeavor.

From idea to fruition,
It is not just wishing,
But hard work, dedication and time,
To make this manuscript come together, align.

Open Up To Writing

(Quatrain)
10/02/2021

Make yourself sit down and write.
Do not fear or get up tight.
Let the words within you flow.
Write about something you know.

It will become easier,
As concepts develop sure.
Open up your mind and see,
Where it goes as you journey.

It is just a simple task,
Put to paper, make it last.
You will be glad that you tried.
Practice will make your work strive.

Story Funnel

(Progressive Snowball)
11/15/2021

Two more poems will make it eighty.
Keep the rhythm of your story.
Tell it now with fanfare glory.
Technique gives it structure, body.

Show how you write as you go.
Let it ebb and let it flow.
Add some depth to layers, show,
How your characters can grow.

Put yourself inside.
Do not your traits hide.
Set your doubts aside.
Let your story thrive.

Shorter vision.
Micro fiction.

Let me see,
That story.

Ode To Original Writing

(Ode)
10/02/2021

Make a plan to write something.
Ideas, concepts to it bring.
Shape it, morph it, something new.
Give it life as written true.

Let your ideas ebb and flow,
Maybe fast or maybe slow,
It will develop into shape,
As you care with it take.

Let your soul expel its breath.
As you add words to express,
What you feel inside yourself.
Do not leave it on a shelf.

Take away your jitters, fears.
Let your heart shine through your tears.
There is nothing more beautiful,
Than a work original.

The Last Poem

(Couplet)
11/15/2021

Should this be the last poem?
Where is this story going?

Have I showed you technique,
To make your story unique?

You don't need a tissue.
Do not force the issue.

We are by no means through.
There is more to come in twenty twenty–two.

Let your stories flow naturally.
No need to doubt bashfully.

With your own style and flair,
Craft it with good care.

If writing is your ability,
To share it is your legacy.

www.ingramcontent.com/pod-product-compliance
Lightning Source LLC
Chambersburg PA
CBHW071904070526
44583CB00016B/1837